I0881714

VISION and VOICE

An Art-Making Journal for Teens

68 INVITATIONS to Inspire Exploration and Expression

by **Caren Sacks**
Licensed Creative Arts Therapist

To you, holding this journal in your hands.
I hope your journey with *Vision and Voice* allows you the time for yourself for reflection, exploration, calm, and experiencing the magical process of art making.

To Simone Kaplan, whose vision and voice was instrumental in the creation of this journal.
—C.S.

Art making can be a magical process. It can allow you to express yourself—to create images that may be fun or funny, that make you smile, or that remind you of specific times and experiences. Art making can bring joy as you create. In expressing our authentic selves via art making, our difficult and challenging feelings, thoughts, and experiences can also be expressed and explored. It can offer a sense of control, hope, comfort, affirmation of how you are feeling, and so much more. This journal offers a space to express all of your feelings: seeing and knowing them can enable you to address them and perhaps explore and practice shifting from some of the difficult feelings that can hold you back to a kinder, gentler, more compassionate way of understanding your feelings, thoughts, and experiences.

As you flip through your journal, I hope you are inspired
to draw and transform each page.
Art is not perfect. Try not to judge yourself, your art,
or your feelings. Put aside any "shoulds," "can'ts," and "don'ts."
Find the yesses!

Yes to you

Yes to who you are

Yes to your imagination

Yes to exploring and experimenting

Yes to playing and creating

Yes to making art

Yes to your vision

Yes to your voice

YES!

This journal has 68 art-making invitations that are divided into four sections: *About Being Playful, About Me, About Feelings,* and *About Knowing Yourself.* You can use colors, shapes, lines, and collage to represent and express your experiences, thoughts, and feelings. You can create images that are realistic or abstract. An art-making invitation may inspire you to create something different than what is written, and that's okay. Art making can give you the space to discover your vision and listen to and speak your voice.

How to Use this Journal

- ★ Find a comfortable place to create.
- ★ Doodle, scribble, or collage. Your creations can be abstract or realistic. Add words to your drawings if you choose.
- ★ Find a page in the journal you would like to explore and respond to, a page that speaks to you in the moment.
- ★ You may want to share your drawing with someone.
- ★ Express and represent your feelings, thoughts, and experiences.
- ★ Communicate in pictures and images.
- ★ Identify new solutions or new ways to see existing challenges.
- ★ Practice self-compassion.
- ★ Have fun while creating.

Important to Note

As you engage with the art-making invitations in this journal, you may experience feelings of being present and grounded, as well as learn new ways to understand and respond to challenging situations, thoughts, or feelings. These, along with relaxation and a sense of calm, are healing benefits of art making and creativity.

However, if you are struggling with feelings that challenge you in different areas of your daily life—that make it difficult to sleep, pay attention in school, or spend time with your family and friends—or if your thoughts and feelings include hurting yourself, someone else, or your environment, you need to speak to a therapist or counselor.

Therapy is a form of self-care. You may be surprised by how many teens are in therapy—it's more common than you may think. You may have friends or family members who have been involved in therapy as a way to address and support a variety of concerns and challenges.

There are different kinds of therapy: traditional talk therapy, drama therapy, music therapy, art therapy, and therapies that focus on a specific therapeutic technique or practice. It is important to find a therapist that is a good fit for you. Your parent, caregiver, pediatrician, or school counselor can help you find one.

Everyone needs a place to share their feelings and experiences and have someone to listen and support them. Take good care of yourself!

Additional art-making invitations can be found on my website,
www.carensacks.com

Suggested art materials

Oil pastels, colored pencils, markers that won't bleed through the page, and crayons are all great choices to use in this journal. You can also collage with paper, magazine pictures and words, and a glue stick—use whatever materials you most enjoy creating with.

An additional sketchbook is handy if you want to respond to any of the invitations more than once, to create on a different size paper, or to use materials that would be more suitable for heavier paper.

About Being Playful: Art making for playing, exploring, and experimenting.

This is *your* journal. What would you like to draw on this first page? You can play with colors, shapes, and lines. You can experiment with different materials. You can create playful images or calming images. You can draw something abstract or realistic. You can create anything you choose!

Scribbling can be a great way to warm up when beginning a drawing. Use this page to scribble, with as many or as few colors as you'd like. Sometimes you can see or find something in your scribble that reminds you of something you can draw. And sometimes, a scribble is just a scribble. There are so many ways to scribble—you can scribble fast or slow, big or small, with your eyes closed, or with your nondominant hand. You can draw a scribble that's calm, frustrated, happy, angry, or another feeling. There is no pressure to create anything specific. How does it feel to be scribbling?

If it was possible for a wish to be granted, what would you wish for? If granted, what would this wish look like?

This is not a mistake. This page is upside down. What does it inspire you to draw?

If you had a superpower, what would it be? What would it look like? What would you be able to do? You can draw your superpower.

Do you use emojis when you text or write? You can create your own personal emoji. What does it look like? What does it say about you?

If you created an app, what would it do? What would it look like? What would you name it? You can draw what your app looks like and what it offers.

You can draw along to a favorite song, listening to the music and lyrics. As you listen, you can experiment using both your dominant and nondominant hand.

A mandala is a circle. Drawing inside a mandala can be soothing and centering. A mandala can contain one's stress and anxiety or represent one's joy and delight. Draw within a circle to create your own mandala.

Think of a funny story from when you were younger or a baby. You can draw an image from the story you remember or one you were told about.

What inspires you? You can draw a picture of what inspiration looks and feels like for you.

You can draw a picture using your favorite colors. How do you feel creating it and looking at the finished drawing?

Smiling and laughing can feel so good! What are some things that make you smile or laugh? You can create a picture that makes you smile or laugh.

About Me: Art making about who you are, your experiences, responses, and relationships.

Having a place where we feel safe is important to all of us. Think of this place—it can be real or from your imagination. You can draw the place where you feel safe. You can include anything that helps you feel safe.

How do you feel when you wake up in the morning? Are you grumpy, excited for a new day, still sleepy, or something else? You can draw a picture of how you feel when you wake up in the morning.

What does your best day look and feel like? It can be real or imagined. What makes it the best? You can draw what your best day looks like.

What does your worst day look and feel like? It can be real or imagined. What makes it the worst? You can draw what your worst day looks like.

Moving your body by dancing, exercising, running, and jumping can feel energizing, tiring, calming, or something else. You can draw how you feel after moving.

We can be thankful for many things: our family, our friends, or our pets. Maybe you are thankful for something in your room or your house. Perhaps there is a moment in history or an invention that you are thankful for. What are you thankful for? What does feeling thankful look and feel like?

We all can sometimes be judgmental, even though we may try not to be. What kind of things are you judgmental about? You can draw how it feels to be judgmental, and perhaps what it might look like to let go of those judgments.

Do you have a core group of people you count on? Your circle of support may include family members, friends, and some teachers and coaches. Who are these people? How does it feel to talk to them, be with them, do activities with them? You can draw your circle of support.

We all dream when we sleep. Sometimes we remember our dreams, sometimes we don't. You can draw a dream that you remember. Is it one that made you smile, or was it confusing or scary? You can draw how you would like to alter or change the dream, perhaps by giving it a different ending. If it would be helpful to share with someone, do so.

You can draw an image of something important or an event that happened to you today. It can be something big or small. What is it, and what does it look like?

Do you have a favorite quote that inspires or comforts you? It can be one that you created yourself or one from someone else. You can write the quote and illustrate it.

If others could really see you, understand you, know you, and accept you, what would you like them to see? You can draw an image of how you would like others to *really* see you.

Do you have a playlist of your favorite music? You can create the cover art for your playlist.

It's easy to think of the things we don't do well. Take some time to think of the things that you do well. What are they? Celebrate these strengths and create an image that reflects them.

If you were planning your own birthday celebration, what would it look like? How do you like to celebrate your birthday?

What does your relationship with your family look and feel like? It may be just right for you, or it maybe different than what you wish for or feel you need. You can draw your relationship with your family as it is or as you would like it to be. If it would it be helpful to share this with a member of your family, do so.

When you have a problem, are going through a difficult time, or are struggling with something, what does help look like? Does it include someone offering possible solutions, quiet support and encouragement, a hug, or something different? You can draw a picture of what help and support looks like for you.

About Feelings: Art making to identify, explore, and express your feelings.

We experience many different feelings. Here is a list of some of them.

Angry, anxious, annoyed, ambitious, belonging, brave, calm, capable, compassionate, competent, confident, confused, curious, disappointed, embarrassed, empathic, envious, excited, fearful, frustrated, giddy, glad, gratitude, grief, guilty, happy, honored, hopeful, hopeless, humiliated, hurt, inspired, jealous, joyful, judgmental, lonely, loving, moody, optimistic, overwhelmed, pleased, proud, regret, restful, sad, safe, scared, serious, shame, shy, silly, sorry, strong, surprised, thrilled, trustful, vulnerable, worried.

What makes you happy? You can draw what feeling happy looks like for you. A visual reminder of what makes you feel happy may help when you are feeling sad.

You can draw a time you thought you couldn't do something, but you did it anyway. How did it feel, and what does it look like?

Negative thoughts get in the way of many things: our relationships with family and friends, doing well in school, and how we feel about ourselves. Negative self-talk is critical, judgmental, and unkind. It can increase stress and anxiety and can come between you and your goals. Positive self-talk is kind, caring, and understanding. It can support you through difficult and challenging times. It can motivate you as well. When you practice positive self-talk, it sounds like talking to a good friend. You can draw a picture of how it feels to practice positive self-talk. Include words of support and encouragement if you like.

Our bodies can give us clues about how we are feeling. Do you blush? Do your muscles tense up? Do your palms get sweaty? Do you get butterflies in your stomach? Do you feel your heart beating faster? Do you get teary? Or something else? You can draw how your body lets you know how you are feeling and what that looks like. Identifying how you are feeling is helpful.

We express anger in many ways: yelling, stamping our feet, slamming a door, being mean to someone, or something else. You can draw what anger looks like for you. After drawing anger, how do you feel? Does drawing about it help it dissipate? Did your anger drawing surprise or scare you? If you like, alter this drawing, or create another one that speaks to managing your anger.

What makes you smile, giggle, and roll on the floor laughing? You can draw what makes you laugh and how it feels.

There are days when things don't go as planned. How does that feel? What does it look like? What can you try to get back on track? What does that look and feel like?

Remember a time you did something kind or thoughtful for someone. You can draw what that looks like and how it feels.

We all need coping skills to help us with challenging feelings and experiences. You can draw and write what your coping skills are. They may include taking a break, going for a walk, listening to music, drawing in this journal, having a healthy snack, talking to a friend, and/or practicing deep breathing. You can create an image of how it feels when you practice coping skills and what you do to feel less stressed, frustrated, or overwhelmed.

Frustration—we all experience it. You can draw how frustration looks and feels to you. Consider changing or altering your drawing to reflect what happens when you practice coping skills.

Perhaps you want to feel different than you feel in this moment. You can draw yourself feeling the way you would like to.

Do you worry before a test, a presentation, or before doing something new? You can try transforming your worry by drawing yourself feeling positive and strong.

What does joy look like? How does it feel in your body? You can draw your joy.

Our feelings change throughout the day. Sometimes we experience more than one feeling at a time. You can draw some of the feelings you experienced today. You might not have the words to identify how you are feeling, but you may be able to find the colors or shapes that feel right. When you are finished with the drawing, you may be able to name your feelings or you may not.

We all experience anxiety sometimes—it's part of life. What resources/coping skills do you have? What are some you want to develop? What does managing your anxiety look and feel like?

When we are scared, angry, or worried, taking big, slow breaths or being aware of our breath as we inhale and exhale can help us calm down. You can practice any breathing techniques that work for you. What colors and shapes are your breaths? You can draw how it feels to pay attention to your breath and what it looks like.

Apologizing can be hard. It can mean we've made a mistake—that we said, did, or forgot to do or say something. How does it feel and what does it look like when you apologize to someone?

What does love look and feel like to you?

We all worry about things sometimes. You can create a picture of what your worry looks and feels like. You can also explore and draw what helps when you worry. You can alter or change your worry to look and feel different.

Think of the list of feelings and emotions from the beginning of this section. Does one fit how you are feeling now, or how you would like to feel now? Draw what that feeling looks or feel like. You can also create an image of any other feeling or feelings.

About Knowing Yourself: Art-making invitations that speak to your experiences, stories, vision, and voice.

Do you ever get so involved in art, music, cooking, or some other activity that you lose track of time? This is called being in the flow. It can be relaxing and focusing. What kinds of things allow you to experience being in the flow? You can draw what being in the flow looks and feels like for you.

Is there an issue, in the world or your community, that you would like to do something about? It can be something small. What does getting involved look and feel like for you?

There are things we can control and things we can't. You can draw something you cannot control and something that you can.

We all make mistakes. What does making mistakes look like? What can you learn from mistakes? What does that look like?

What is something you are grateful for? Is it a person, animal, place, thing, or something else? You can create an image that shows what you are grateful for or what gratitude looks like for you.

What are some of your dreams, plans, and goals for your future? You can create an image using words, shapes, and colors to imagine what your future would look like in six months, a year, or even five years from now.

Is there an obstacle in your way? What does it look like? How big is it? How can you address it? How can you go over, around, under, or through it? What does it look like to overcome the obstacle?

We all face challenges, both big and small. They can be related to school, peers, family members, your goals. or to something else. You can create an image that shows your challenge and what it looks like when you acknowledge and address it.

How do you feel about social media and the role it plays in your everyday life? What control do you have over your involvement in social media? You can express your feelings and experiences with social media through drawing.

Do you have concerns, questions, or situations you would like to share with a parent or trusted adult about yourself or a friend that you aren't able to find the words or courage to discuss? What do these concerns look like? You can draw them and consider sharing your art to help begin the conversation with your parent or trusted adult.

Your imagination is pretty awesome. It allows you to see new things and remember old things. It allows you to develop new ideas, thoughts, and images. Your imagination is limitless. It can surprise you with beautiful images. It can also take you to dark places. We can use our imagination to shed light onto those dark places. You can encourage your imagination to shift so you can see alternatives. You can draw an image from your imagination that supports the statement, "I've got this." It's something we all need to practice. What does "I've got this" look like for you?

Being outside in nature can help clear one's mind. When you paint or draw what you see when you are in nature, it's called "plein air." You can take your journal outside to draw what you see.

You can draw or illustrate a story. It can be a real event or something from your imagination. What do you want to include in your story? Is there a message in your story? Would you like to share your story and drawing with someone? If so, who is that person?

Self-compassion is so important to practice, yet it can be difficult. It's easy to be hard on ourselves and to say mean, harsh things, things we would never say to others. Self-compassion and positive self-talk are a form of self-care. We need to practice talking to ourselves as we would when we are supporting a friend. You can draw what self-compassion looks and feels like for you.

What does relaxation look and feel like for you? You can draw what relaxation looks like for you.

"Courage doesn't always roar. Sometimes courage is the little voice at the end of the day that says, 'I'll try again tomorrow,'" states author Mary Ann Radmacha. You can create a drawing that speaks to your courage about trying again tomorrow.

You are almost at the last page of this journal. Did you learn something new about yourself while responding to these art-making invitations? Do you have a new awareness or understanding of something? You can draw about your experience with this journal.

This is the last page in your art-making journal! You can draw a picture of what you liked about this journal and how it feels to be completing it. You can keep drawing in a sketchbook if you like. You can also get additional art-making invitations like these on my website: www.carensacks.com

One More Thing

Some of the art-making invitations in this journal ask you to identify coping skills to use when you may be having a difficult moment or day. Coping skills can be challenging to remember when we need them. Use the list below as a reference and reminder when you need to manage difficult situations, experiences, and feelings. Having a variety of coping skills is helpful—if one doesn't work, you can try another. Feel free to add to this list to make it your own.

1. Use positive self-talk. Talk to yourself as if you were talking to a good friend and being supportive, understanding, and accepting.
2. Practice self-compassion. Be kind to yourself and accept that you're human, which means that you, like the rest of us, are not perfect.
3. Identify how you are feeling in the moment—name it and describe it.
4. Talk with someone you trust—a friend, parent, or other trusted adult.
5. Listen to calming, relaxing music.
6. Draw or write in a journal.
7. Practice deep breathing (or any breathing technique that works for you). For example, find a comfortable place to sit and take some deep breaths. Count to four as you inhale and four as you exhale. Do this again, this time counting to five, then six. Continue breathing with the intention of relaxing.
8. Look around your environment—name something you can see, smell, touch, or taste.
9. Move your body—dance, exercise, or go for a walk.
10. Visualize a calm and relaxing place, either a real or imaginary one.
11. Find funny animal videos or anything that makes you laugh.

AND

12. Create! Draw, paint, collage, work with clay—do whatever art making that works for you!

ABOUT THE AUTHOR

Caren Sacks, MA, ATR-BC, LCAT, ATCS, is a licensed, board certified creative arts therapist and board-certified art therapy supervisor who has been providing clinical services in a variety of settings for more than forty years. She is dedicated to ensuring that people—no matter their age—have an opportunity to explore their creativity and express themselves, both on and off the page. This journal is a result of her experiences in sharing the joys and significance of art making with children, teens, and adults.

You can find out more about Caren and her work at www.carensacks.com

Text and illustrations copyright © 2024 by Caren Sacks. All rights reserved. No part of this journal may be reproduced in any form without written permission from the publisher.

Library of Congress Cataloging-in-Publication Data available.
ISBN: 978-1-68555-731-7
Manufactured in China

MIX
Paper from responsible sources
FSC® C102842

Printed using Forest Stewardship Council certified stock from sustainably managed forests.

Borders by Anne Vahcic.
Design by Semadar Megged.
1 3 5 7 9 10 8 6 4 2

The Collective Book Studio®
Oakland, California
www.thecollectivebook.studio

While the art-making invitations in this journal offer opportunities to draw and talk about your experiences and feelings, please remember it is not therapy or art therapy.

If you are struggling with difficult feelings and worries, you should discuss them with a trusted adult, your pediatrician, or school counselor. Therapy can be helpful when you are struggling to manage your feelings, relationships, or behavior, or if there is a challenging life event or family changes.